These are [illegible] e loss of someone ve[illegible] a warmth too: they sp[illegible] emory of his beloved l[illegible] in everything he says and does. We share his pain, but we also share his love.

Sadie Kaye, author of 'From Earth and Sky'.

Spun From Air and Sunlight's poetry takes you gently by the hand and lets you know it's ok to feel what you feel and that everything is going to be alright. Every line softly caresses the heartstrings and opens a window to worlds we all know. Beautiful, kind and uplifting, this collection carries the ultimate message: it's ok; you are not alone.

Laura Liptrot, author of 'I am not a padlock'.

Thank you for your support!

Spun From Air and Sunlight

Published in England in 2025 by Tenebrous Texts

Edited by Steven C. Davis

1 3 5 7 9 10 8 6 4 2

ISBN 978-1-914246-50-0
Typeset and designed by Tenebrous Texts

The Ocean of Grief

By

Spun From Air and Sunlight

Grief is a very personal thing, everyone who goes through it will experience it differently.
These are my thoughts and feelings after the death of my wife Najma from ovarian cancer on our 31st wedding anniversary:

26th April 2023

30th April 2023

I've loved her.
Held her,
Hand,
And tight all through the night.
We've loved and laughed days away,
Had children and danced with life.
I've been cherished and nursed.
Then I cherished and nursed.
And then she was gone.
I cleaned her and said many prayers,
Carried her one last time
Then laid her to sleep.
And now life goes on.
I feel her everywhere
Memories catch in my tear ducts
Before falling away into light
I've loved her.
I love her.
No more needs to be said.

3rd May 2023

One week.
Passed in an eternal moment.
Since she's gone.
I go through the motions,
Doing what must be done.
But I'm observing,
Not taking part.
Sitting at the side hidden by a teary smile
The dance goes on
Without me for now.
I'll be back
The fierce joy of love lived can't go out.
Sadness enfolds it for now
And I chose to rest,
Catch my breath,
Lest the sobs and tears fall from me,
Until I can see her smile in my mind
And not cry.
It will come,
But for now
I watch the world
Observing.

5th May 2023

Caffeine
In a coffee shop,
Caffeinating my way out of grief.
This will not work. I know it.
I'm not stupid!
But I'm trying anyway
Because,
Because ...
Because there is a strange comfort here.
Here in a shop full of people,
I can sit and be alone.
Alone with my thoughts and
Along with me feelings and
Alone with myself.
Smile and cry and weep,
As emotions carry me along
Like an unstoppable flood
Flowing and flowing
With me in its midst,
One day maybe I'll find a boat,
Learn to navigate again.
But for now,
Caffeine!

13th May 2023

Driving west,
I've found a place,
With trees and flowers
Paths and pools
Deer tracks and wild garlic
She'd love it here.

Crying in a wood is different
The trees hear you
They'll support you if you let them.
A path will lead your feet to beauty.
A bright petal reminds you of times shared.
I still miss her.
I'm still crying

But ...

Crying in a wood is different.

16th May 2023

<u>Sorry</u>

I feel you can feel me,
I'm sorry I'm sad,
But I really really miss you,
And today,
That feels bad.

20th May 2023

Grief is a Sonnet

I've loved you so deeply for thirty one years
We danced ever closer and faced down our fears.
As we grew together, entwining our souls
So we loved each other, achieving our goals.
We made of our lives something solid and strong,
And played to the universe, enjoying our song.
The music goes on but our duet is done,
I'm learning to sing when the music's for one.
There are other singers, our children and friends
They dance their own music, the song never ends
But our dance is over, you've bowed out for now
I'm singing my solo until my last bow.
And when the time comes for my last earthly note
We'll dance back together, and love what we wrote.

25th May 2023

Something is wrong
Because of course, everything is wrong.
I used to know what was next,
Now, I'm not so sure.
Don't worry,
I know some things don't change,
The mortgage, the kids,
Heartbeats.
The bank still has to be fed.
But,
Now you have gone
I'm lost
Adrift,
Passing through.

It's nearly a month already
I don't want the hurting to stop.
It reminds me of you,
In a sad but good way.
Sometimes I cry,
Overwhelmed
By feelings I can't pin down.
I pray for you always.
But something is wrong
Since you left.

30th May 2023

Grief is exhausting.
I don't think that's very fair!
There's loads to do and organise,
And you are just not there.
We used to work together
Sorting life out as a team.
Now the team approach is broken
And I'm living in a dream.
It's not that I'm not coping,
Everything is getting done.
But I have to say quite honestly,
Without you life's much less fun.
We were together for so long
Three decades and 1 year
And now I feel you all the time
That's how I know you're near.
I feel that you can feel my thoughts
So I keep some locked inside.
And I'm so tired,
All the time,
Since,
The night,
You died.

31st May 2023

5 weeks today
Since I held you as you died.
Since the world froze solid in a
moment.
Since I carried on alone.
Since I saw your eyes.
Since I heard you breathing.
Since I held your hand.
Since I sat beside you.
Since I shared a view with you.
Since I could picture you without
crying.
5 weeks today.

I hurt because I love you
In massive surging waves,
And I know you loved me back
For all those lovely days.
"The perfect couple" people said,
And actually they weren't wrong,
We were so good together,
Two halves of the same song.
Our love held us so safely
And made us spin along,
The sparkling river of our life
So happy for so long.
So it hurts now as I'm carried on
Alone in the river's flow,
Because grief is just love
When it has nowhere to go.

8th June 2023

Sitting trying not to cry
In a place we used to go
Listening to the chatter
Of lunches eaten slow.
I remember that you used to love
The tea-bread buttered well.
They haven't got it on today
So on the cakes I start to dwell
But I hear your voice inside my head
A quiet admonition,
And order mushroom soup instead
Cos it's best for my nutrition.
You should be sitting with me now
That's how it's meant to be.
I don't understand how to do things
When you're not here to see.
I'm trying really really hard
To keep going day by day
And make sure that I don't discard
Any help along the way.
I promise that I will not fall
You do not need to worry.
I'm still here, upright, standing tall,
But emotions come on in a flurry
Roaring through my heart and bones
Catching me quite by surprise,
And then leave me,
Sitting all alone.
With tears in my eyes.

13th June 2023

Sunlight sparkles on the leaves,
Like fireworks lighting up the trees.
Shadows cool festoon the earth,
And clouds rush by, giving birth,
To images of far off lands,
Then roll and change like shifting sands.
The drowsy insects buzz about,
And far away a buzzard shouts.
Yet underneath it I can hear,
The rolling ocean ever near.
A sound that fills the noiseless void,
And calls me back to ties enjoyed,
Sitting, walking, holding hands,
The joy of two in loving lands.

21st June 2023

I don't know what do.
That isn't very nice.
I'm feeling lost and tired and sad,
In need of some advice.
But the person that I turn to,
Whenever I feel down,
Has gone and gone forever,
Way more than out of time.
To think of her is all I do,
Her smile, her piercing eyes,
Of her wise words and warm embrace
And inside me something cries.
I'm feeling lost and tired and sad
That isn't very nice
You see,
I don't know what to do,
Now she's in paradise.

23rd June 2023

I wake up,
And think of you.
Get washed,
And think of you.
Pray,
And think of you.
Eat breakfast,
And think of you.
Fill my day,
And think of you.
Cry by your grave,
And think of you.
Come home,
And think of you.
Have my tea,
And think of you.
Got to bed,
And think of you.
I wake up ...

Portholland, Cornwall

28th June 2023
Portholland Cornwall

There's a glamour in the ocean,
A whisper in the sea,
The waves that crash upon the rocks,
Are calling out to me.
I listen most intently
To the messages they send.
I know I need to hear them
Speak of storms that end.
Of sunrise burning brightly
And foam upon the shore,
The laughter and the happiness
That I have known before.
That whisper from the ocean
Is a sound that's always near,
In every silent moment
It's ringing in my ear.
That stationary movement
Of waves upon the shore,
Is constant, never ending
With the power to reassure.
It tells me that the world goes on,
And that my life must too.
So I'll sit a while and listen
While my thoughts return to you.

29th June 2023

I'm learning to live
In a world without you,
Where I'm doing for one
What we once did for two.
I miss you so much
And it's making me cry.
But the world does go on
Even when your love dies.
I want to be with you,
To hold you so tight,
To kiss you and listen
As you breathe through the night.
I keep wanting to show you
The beauty I've found,
Finding joy was so easy
When you were around.
I pray and I pray
And I hope that you hear,
And see through my eyes,
Past every tear.
I'm living for you now,
So life will go on
I'm learning how life works
When two become one.

4th July 2023
Out of order?

I'm feeling lost,
I make plans,
But the tide turns,
The waves erase,
And I am left
Bereft.

It's too big,
This ocean of grief,
Fills my heart
My soul.
It leaves no room
For thought,
For plan.
And I am left
Bereft.

I will not drown,
Will not sink in downward spiral
To despair down there
In the stark dark.
But I am left Bereft.

You have gone
I swim on
Continue without you
Because
I am left
Bereft.

10th July 2023

My life has broken.
The keystone is gone,
The pieces crashed to the floor.
I can't put it back together.
Because a piece has gone forever.
So I survey the wreckage,
Try to find a new structure
A new way
For the pieces to fit together.
But I keep finding holes,
Places where you used to be.
Awkward angles that no longer match.
So I survey the wreckage.
Start again.
I'll keep trying,
But it's hard,
It's hard when I need you,
To help me hold it together.
So
I survey the wreckage ...

15th July 2023

I missed you today, and yesterday,
And the day before, and the day before,
But you know that.
I love you, and that doesn't change,
Because you went away,
Because you died.
That's not how it works.
I pick up a rock and put it in my pocket.
Holding it feels like holding your hand,
As we walk together.
I know that sounds ridiculous.
Your hands were soft,
and warmed in my pocket as I held them,
Like a rock, absorbing body heat.
The hurting is good,
It tells me I'm alive,
That I still love you.
I don't want it to stop.
I don't want to "feel better".
I can still be happy, still laugh
Find joy in the world,
Around the edges.
But the middle?
The middle still loves you.
As it should.

My brain has emptied
Emotions draining through eyes
And mouth
And stomach.
Leaving an empty vessel,
Breathing
Hearing
From behind
The invisible wall.
Apart
Not a part
I go on
Frozen in place

23rd July 2023
Later

"I want it now!"
A toddler screams
"Not later!"
Tears and tantrums
Exploding.
They don't understand,
Can't process
In their newly minted mind
That 'later' is a thing.
For them there is just 'before' and 'now'.

'Later' just means 'not now'.

I want you back
I want you now!
But I'm all grown up
So I don't scream
Don't wail and stamp my feet.
Even if I want to.
But I pray so hard,
Silently screaming.
Hoping someone can hear.
Believing as hard as I can.
Please,
Please!

Let 'later' be a thing.

1st September 2023
To do

Today I will:
Sort out my life
Start the diet
Get more exercise
Find a new job
Get enough sleep
Work on my hobby
Start that new book
Plan out the day
Paint the bathroom
Cut the hedge
Bake some bread
Work on my social skills
Not cry

And

Forget that you died.

29th December 2023

Breathing Underwater

I'm breathing underwater,
Waves rolling overhead.
I'm breathing underwater,
My world's changed now you're dead.
I'm breathing underwater,
Learning to adapt.
I'm breathing underwater,
And I am still intact.
I'm breathing underwater,
Coping with the changes.
I'm breathing underwater,
As my spirit rearranges.
I'm breathing underwater,
As I learn to live with grief.
I'm breathing underwater,
Though it stretches my belief.
I'm breathing underwater,
Changed beyond compare.
I'm breathing underwater,
But it's still me, way down there.

18th May 2024

I came to the end,
Of day, and road, and land.
The waves whispered,
A secret sound settled,
Inside the roar.
A choir of droplets,
Singing one message to my soul,
"We miss her too."

As the sun sinks
Into cotton wool comfort,
The sky burns with cool pink fire,
The sea takes the colour,
Mixing and blending,
A lilac ocean
Curls before me.

Her favourite colour
Shines,
From soaking sand
To far horizon.
"See, we love her too!"
The ocean choir laments
As a wind begins to blow.

18th June 2024
The Widower

A little boy sits in the long grass,
Finding patterns in the leaves,
Making pictures with daisies and dandelions,
Telling himself stories to pass the day,
Hoping the big boys won't see him.
He knows his way home,
But is lost because the path has gone away.
How could that happen?
How could it be the reliable road,
Back to happiness and safety,
Could just go away?
He feels the grass and the sun on his back,
He sees the patterns all around him,
And it all looks the same,
But how can the path be gone?
He feels lonely and scared,
So he distracts himself with stories,
Of adventure and love and success.
He tells himself it will be alright,
He can find his way without the path.
He CAN!
He will,
But, the safe, loving path,
That he has known for so long,
Has vanished into the past.
How can the path be gone?

8th July 2024

It isn't fair!
That you died.
We were so good together,
Facing the world arm in arm.
So it isn't fair!
That you had to leave.

31 years of marriage,
Of deliriously, gloriously
Happy marriage!
Our souls entwined,
Tributaries becoming a river.

It just isn't fair!
You completed me,
Two halves of the same apple,
Your insight stopping or starting me,
Leading me along the best path,
Finding wonder in the world,
Opening my eyes.

It isn't fair,
That all people can't have,
What I had with you.

It isn't fair
But I'm very glad
We were us.

17th July 2024

Pointless
Experiences flood through me,
Joyful, ecstatic experiences,
Opening my eyes to the wonder,
Of all creation.

Pointless
Insight hits me like a train,
Deep understanding of the system,
The network of life and Earth and Universe
Revealed
To my awestruck understanding.

Pointless
Activity occupies me,
Learning to create and explore,
Finding talents that were hidden inside,
For a lifetime.

Pointless
Excitement fires my mind and body,
I vibrate with possibility,
With extraordinary energy
I long to share with you,

But that's pointless,

You died.

23rd July 2024
In the Garden

I've finished my coffee,
Sitting here,
Alone in our garden,
For the first time
Since.
Since ...
Since you died.

I remember
You gently smiling over a cup of tea,
Sitting in the chair next to me,
Chatting about our day.

I remember,
Lockdown afternoons,
"Working from home"
At the garden table,
Laptop open,
You reading a magazine,
Side by side,
Our knees touching,
Ever so slightly.

I remember
Lying on the trampoline,
Watching the cloud animals go by,
My arm under your shoulders,
A blanket covering us,
Safe, warm,
Together.

I remember,
Collecting the tulip pots together.
By the window,
And how happy it made you
That you could see them,
One last time.

I remember
How much you loved this garden,
And gently,
Wipe the tears
From my eyes.

12:24
16.0 KB/S
79
QR & Barcode Sca...
Authenticator
The Fika app
eBay
ebay
1

7th August 2024

I Have Your Picture

I have your picture on my phone,
Your soft smile and piercing eyes
Seeing straight into my soul
With every look.
In a moment, I'm with you,
Arms and heart filled with your love,
With you I want nothing,
Need nothing,
Completed by your presence
I find myself,
In Heaven.

Together we lived our dreams into
Reality.
Faced storms and droughts,
Endured and grew stronger,
Took on our demons
And defeated them,
One, by one.

"I love you."
So inadequate a phrase,
To express a bond,
So achingly beautiful,
So deep a part
Of who we were
Of who I am.

Now you have gone,
Your trials ended,
Life's mission complete.
I carry you,
Inside the best of me,
The me,
That we created together,
And,
I have your picture,
On my phone.

7th September 2024
This is Not a Sentence

Flat,
Suppressed,
Held in,
Pressurised.
Rigid,
Unthinking,
Occupied,
Busy.
Waiting,
Filling,
Resisting,
Overflowing,
Bursting,
Collapsing,
Weeping.
Facing,
Acknowledging,
Accepting,
Grieving,
And,

Finally,

Feeling.

30th November 2024

A Tense Change

Yesterday, after busying,
I sat down,
Ate my tea
In front of the TV.
It felt,
Normal.
When I realised,
I was scared.
What was happening?
How could 'normal'
Not have you in it?
Then it hit me,
This was normal.
This was how it is
From now on.
The emptiness of that truth
Echoed around me.
Then I felt you,
Drawing me inwards,
To dance
In a sunlit meadow.
To run and laugh,
As the children,
We always were.
Then I realised,
This is how we are now,
And I am happy.

Fear and Potential

I am afraid,
Of failure,
Of not being enough,
Of being inadequate,
Incompetent,
Unable to do.
I wonder,
Why?
But, perhaps,
(best not to commit …)
That is the wrong question.
Perhaps,
(Say it quietly …)
This is normal.
What if fear, is normal?
What if fear, is good?
What if the problem
Is not the fear but our,
(Ahem, let's not depersonalise)
Sorry,
What if the problem
Is not the fear but *my*
Reaction to that fear?
What if the pain
Paralysis and dread,
Are just misunderstood?
What if fear
Is excitement
In the wrong frame?
Framed with joy,
With exuberant positivity
Fear is just a call to action,
A pointer to where
My effort is required.
A reminder that perfection,
Is unattainable,
But that whatever happens,
I'll handle it.
So I accept my fear,
And use it
To guide me
As I keep stepping
Onward,
Saying yes
And moving,
Towards the light …

11th March 2025

Error 404
Operating system resources unavailable.
Executive function failure.
Required memory capacity absent.
Decision matrix locked.
Overwhelm!
Overwhelm!
Overwhelm!
Shut down.

Coffee, food,
Pause, space,
Prayers and tears,
Remembrance.

Reboot
Function restored,
System capacity,
Acceptable.
Normal operation functions,
Available.

Warning – power levels low,
Recharge will be required,
Soon.

15th March 2025

I said yes,
To an unexpected,
Apparently random,
Invitation.
A decision,
Made on the spur of the moment,
That led to wonder.
I said yes,
And, accompanied by friends,
Climbed a mountain.
It was hard!
Step after step,
Upwards,
Drawing energy,
Sucking air,
Leaving me gasping,
My heart racing,
Muscles quivering,
With relentless demand.

But I said yes,
To my own pace,
Pausing often to recoup,
Oxygen demanded by effort,
I kept going.
Finally a scrambling climb,
New muscles working,
Drawing me higher,
Defying an entire planet's gravity,
To lift me to the peak.
I gazed out
Across the whole world,
And was grateful,
I said yes.

We Said Yes

We said yes,
Thrown together by fate,
By ridiculously unlikely
circumstance,
We said yes
To an impossible dream.

We said yes,
And began the climb.
Never wavering from our goal,
Together we were relentless,
Unstoppable.

Our souls entwining so
completely,
We had no choice,
Yes was the only answer
To the offer made by the
universe,
By God.

We faced obstacles,
Fearful tasks,
That felt,
Impossible,
But we believed,

And kept climbing.
There were many pauses,
Moments of reflection,
Of recovery and rest,
But we could see the path,
And we followed it,
Until one day
In front of our witnesses,
And full of exhausted joy,
We attained the goal,
And, together forever,
We said,
Yes.

22nd April 2025

On the 26th April 1992
WE said yes.
Yes to life together,
Yes to the thrills,
And the heartaches,
Yes to living our lives,
Together.

I still have your ring
On my finger,
A symbol of heaven,
The heaven I lived
With you.

On the 26th April 2023
31 years later,
To the day,
You died.
That hurts,
Like falling from grace,
Into eternal fire.

But I still wear your ring,
Because,
It was worth it.

For 31 years, to the day,
I knew heaven.
The light of love
You lit in me
Burns on.
Unquenchable
Through the tears,
The light of love
That we created
Together
Leads me on,
Inside myself
To where you are,
Always a part of me,
A strength at my core
That will not fail.

All things change,
A husband
Becomes a widow,
Learning to follow the light,
And saying yes,
With you
Forever.

9th January 2025

An Unexpected Turn

An unexpected turn,
Of events,
Has sent me spinning,
Flying off the road
I thought I knew so well.
The car is wrecked,
So I sit and consider,
Options.
Return to the security
Of the road,
With a new car
I can continue the journey.
But that turn …
Suddenly I'm not sure
That road leads
To where I want to be.
Perhaps it would be better,
To start walking,
To find connections
To the wild world
I'm surely a part of.
To accept

I don't yet know
My destination.
To go back to the map,
With open eyes,
Decide what really matters,
And take the first steps,
Because,
Events
Took an unexpected turn.

A Red Kite in heaven

23rd April 2025

We all die.
A truth we avoid,
Not wanting to think of,
Absence.

But, it is true,
We do all die,
Sooner or later
We hit the ground,
Passing our molecules on
To future life.

We are all falling,
Hurtling through our lives,
Towards the inevitable
Full stop.

Which means,
We all have a choice.
To say NO!
To scream and thrash,
"To rage against the dying of the light!"
As a better poet than me
Once said.

Or not.

We can choose,
To say yes,
To enjoy the flight,
To open our arms and hearts,
To sing and be blown away
By the exhilaration of the wind.

It really is that simple.
So, Yes, or No,
Which will you choose?

Surviving the Ocean of Grief

This is a series of 5 poems that I wrote between 24th June and 23 July 2023. They are meant to describe the different states I found myself in after Najma died on the 26th April. It is very important to realise that although they could be interpreted as "stages of grief" that I passed through one after the other, that is absolutely not how I experienced them. I found myself moving from one state to another and back again repeatedly as my emotional state swung around over the months. There were moments when I fell all the way back to Part 1 and others where I found myself looking forward and trying to sort my new life out as described in Part 5 but those states could both be on the same day!

Everyone's experience of grief is unique, just as every love is unique, so this is not meant to be an instruction manual, it's just a description of what grief felt like for me at that moment. If you recognise yourself in some of the words, I hope there is some comfort in seeing the feelings expressed this way.

24th June 2023 – 23rd July 2023

Surviving the Ocean of Grief
Part 1: Immersion

Go under.
Don't fight it.
You can't win.
Let it come.
Ripping up
Through stomach
Heart and lungs,
Let tears fall
And wracking sobs convulse you.
The pain you feel,
That rips you into pieces
That consumes you
That blots out air
And speech and thought
Like a wave crashing
Tumbling you along
Helpless.
You have to feel it.
Acknowledge it's there.
Be brave,
Don't fight it.
Go under.

Surviving the Ocean of Grief
Part 2: Survival Float

Waves pass,
Convulsions end,
Head up, take a breath.
Relax,
Relax
Just for a moment.
The next wave is coming,
To crash over you
And spin you helpless,
Again underwater.
But now you know.
You know it will pass.
You will breathe again.
Wait for the pause,
The brief moments
Of calm and clarity.
Know they are coming,
As surely as the next wave,
As surely as the overwhelming
Awful pain.
Let it come again,
Let it pour from you.
The wave will pass
Head up,
Take a breath.

Surviving the Ocean of Grief
Part 3: Backstroke

Act.
Do something,
Anything.
With feet and hands
And head.
Direction doesn't matter.
Occupy yourself,
Kick, Reach, Kick, Reach,
The waves will still come.
Kick, Reach, Kick, Reach.
You will tire,
Will need survival float again.
That doesn't matter.
Just act.
Kick out of place
Your misery, your pain.
Carry them with you.
Reach for anyone, anything
Anywhere, to fill time.
Direction doesn't matter.
Kick, Reach, Kick, Reach
You can't see where you're going,
It doesn't matter.
Kick, Reach, Kick, Reach.
Any thing.
Any one,
Any where
Just act.
Please.

Surviving the Ocean of Grief
Part 4: Treading Water

The storm is behind you,
Still there on the horizon,
Waiting for a stray thought,
A memory, or passing comment,
To whirl you back
Into chaos and pain.
But,
For now,
The sea is calmer.
An ocean swell
With highs and lows,
Holds you lightly.
Hands and feet move gently,
Lifting your head up.
You have time to look,
Survey the scene,
Identify the reefs and shoals
Where the waves break
With renewed fury.
Time to see the deeper waters.
The gentle swells.
To plot a route.
To find a way forward.
The storm will return,
Take you back to the beginning
But now you know.
Now you know.
There is a way through.

Surviving the Ocean of Grief
Part 5: Choices

Losing them changes everything.
You can rage against the loss,
The ocean, the unbearable injustice,
Of a world without them in it.
Cry in anguished denial,
Spiral down into deep despair
And darkness.

Or not.

Everything is different,
The world is NOT the same.
So now, take time.
Take time to listen.
Listen.
To the message the universe is sending.
Look for the signs,
The brightest star,
The gentle breeze,
The warmer water
Gently caressing your body.
Find a direction,
One that feels right,
Not comfortable,
Or safe
But right.
The world is different.
So find your new direction,
And swim.

Our first picture together as a couple, July 1990.

The last picture of us together October 2022.

About the poet

Hello!
I was born on 6th July 1969 and grew up on the edge of the little town of Nuneaton in Warwickshire. After a frankly idyllic childhood I went to The Polytechnic Wolverhampton to study Biology and Plant Ecology which is where I met my wife Najma. In 1992 I graduated, got married and began a job at the Agricultural Development Advisory Service (ADAS) plant clinic which was my dream job, 1992 was a very good year! After working there for 13 years having 3 children and living life to the full, I moved into teaching, first in secondary school for 7 years then at Dudley College where I currently teach the Access to Higher Education Program.
After Najma was diagnosed in 2021 life became a blur of surgery, chemotherapy and consultant visits. Fitting all that in alongside full time work was impossible so it was wonderful to have the support of Najma's best friend Sara who looked after Naj way better than any nurse could have done and Steph – a survivor of cancer herself who gave her the most wonderful gift pack "for whenever it was needed". Because we were blessed with such lovely friends it was only in January that I had to stop working and go on leave for 6 months. Najma died in April and I am grateful to the college for supporting me in taking the leave I needed before returning to work in September.

When people ask me what I do I usually reply "I'm a teacher" but very, very slowly I'm starting to add "and a poet."

Finally!
All life is intimately connected; plants take in carbon dioxide from the atmosphere and use the power of the sun's rays to break it into carbon and oxygen. The oxygen is discarded and allows all of us to breath whilst the carbons are strung together to make long chains that make up the proteins, carbohydrates, fats and DNA that make up the plant's cells. We in turn eat the plants and use those chains to make our own bodies. So in a very real, scientifically accurate way, we are all made from filaments of air, spun together with sunlight.

I think that's magical.

Spun from Air and Sunlight, August 2025

More poetry from Tenebrous Texts:

'I am not a padlock' – Laura Liptrot

'Every journey starts with the first step and before the first step, unlock the door ... Journey through every season, meeting gods and goddesses, dancing with faeries; dining with kings and water lords.

I am an open door. Read me. Share me, because I am not a padlock.

'All the Colours of the Night' – Lorna Rose

Shameless nature worship, exquisite dissections of desire, a waitress at the end of the world, Lorna Rose's second collection has her trademark candid style, luminous explorations of the connections between the earthly and the spiritual and homages to artists who have continued to inspire her.

'From Earth and Sky' – Sadie Kaye

This book retells much of the Norse mythology of Thor, Odin, Loki and others, drawing on careful research based on original texts and academic commentaries on them. The text is written in beautiful alliterative verse inspired by the original Icelandic sources and is structured around a dialogue between Tyr and Jord. Illustrated with Sadie Kaye's own lino prints based on original Viking art.

'Freshly dipped and bleeding love' – Steven C. Davis

Davis' debut poetry collection is a personal and poignant journey through depression and love, change and growth, a clear political stance 'I stand for Trans' and so much more. Written for and closely aligned to the act of performance, these pieces stand on their own, tearing at the heart strings and challenging us to think upon them further.

Printed in Dunstable, United Kingdom

71604513R10037